ALSO BY CHRIS STORY

The Backyard Millionaire
Born to Live
The Millionaire Maker

Thriller Mystery Books by Chris Story
The Making of Mann
The Watchmann

The Backyard Millionaire Creed

Promise yourself

To invest in yourself

To honor your instincts

To never invest on
an emotional basis

To negotiate with
win/win in mind

To find a need and fill it

Promise yourself
to persist until you win

THE MILLIONAIRE CODE

Unlocking the Principles for Lasting Wealth

CHRIS STORY

Copyright © 2025 Chris Story

All rights reserved. No part of this book may be used or reproduced by any means, graphic, electronic, or mechanical, including photocopying, recording, taping or by any information storage retrieval system without the written permission of the author except in the case of brief quotations embodied in critical articles and reviews.

ISBN (print): 979-8-9852696-7-3
ISBN (ebook): 979-8-9852696-8-0

Story Productions LLC
1005 Carriage Court
Homer Alaska 99603
907.299.7653
AlaskaMattersRadio@gmail.com
www.ILoveHomerAlaska.com

Printed in the United States

For Charles Hough, thank you for handing me a book and a reputation to live up to; I'm in your debt.

CONTENTS

The Backyard Millionaire Creed

Promise yourself

To invest in yourself

To honor your instincts

To never invest on
an emotional basis

To negotiate with
win/win in mind

To find a need and fill it

Promise yourself
to persist until you win

Chapter 1
Promise Yourself

The morning sun spilled through the kitchen window, illuminating the journal in front of August. Its blank pages seemed to mock him, a silent reminder of his frustration. He had been diligent—waking up early, setting goals, visualizing his dreams—but the progress felt painfully slow. No matter how hard he worked, it always seemed like he was one step behind where he wanted to be.

The knock at the door was sharp and familiar. Without waiting for an answer, Oscar let himself in. It was something August had grown used to over the years. Ever since they first met at the hardware store—when August had stubbornly resisted the advice Oscar offered—Oscar had become a fixture in his life, a mentor whose wisdom often arrived uninvited but never unwelcome.

Oscar nodded toward the journal on the table. "Still at it, huh?"

August sighed, pushing the book aside. "Not that it's getting me anywhere. I've been working my tail off, but I'm not making the progress I thought I would. It's like I'm stuck in place."

Oscar pulled a chair out and sat down across from him. He studied August for a moment before reaching into his jacket pocket. "I figured this day would come," he said, unfolding a small, creased piece of paper. "Here. This is for you."

August hesitated before taking it. At the top, in bold letters, were the words *The Backyard Millionaire Creed*. Beneath them was a list of seven simple yet powerful principles.

"Promise yourself," he read aloud, then glanced up at Oscar. "What is this?"

Oscar leaned back, his expression calm. "It's a roadmap. It's how I built everything I have— and how you'll build everything you want. Each of these planks is a promise. You follow them, you commit to them, and I guarantee you'll stop feeling stuck. But it starts with the first one: *Promise yourself*."

August frowned, skeptical. "What does that even mean?"

"It means making a commitment to yourself and taking it seriously," Oscar said. "Think about it. You make promises to other people all the time—your friends, your family, even strangers. And you keep those promises because they matter. But how often do you make a promise to yourself? And when you do, how often do you keep it?"

August sat back, the words sinking in. He thought about the countless times he'd set goals only to abandon them when the path got tough. "But what if I break the promise?"

Oscar gave him a knowing smile. "Then you start over. Every day, you get the chance to recommit. The point isn't perfection, August. It's persistence. When you promise yourself something and truly mean it, you'll find a way to make it happen. That's the difference between wishing for something and building it."

August's eyes drifted back to the creed. He read the first line again: *Promise yourself.* It was so simple, yet it felt like a challenge. Slowly, he reached for his journal.

At the top of the page, he wrote: *I promise myself.* Below it, he began listing his commitments: to trust his instincts, to keep pushing forward, to believe in the vision he'd set for himself.

When he was done, he closed the journal and looked at Oscar. "Alright," he said, his voice steady. "I'll give it a shot."

Oscar stood, a satisfied look on his face. "Good. Stick with it. You'll see the difference soon enough."

As the door clicked shut behind him, August stared at the journal in front of him. For the first time in a long while, the blank pages didn't feel like a burden. They felt like a fresh start.

Oscar's words echoed in his mind: *When you promise yourself something and truly mean it, you'll find a way to make it happen.*

And in that moment, August decided that this promise—to himself—would be one he wouldn't break.

The Backyard Millionaire Creed

Promise yourself

To invest in yourself

To honor your instincts

To never invest on
an emotional basis

To negotiate with
win/win in mind

To find a need and fill it

Promise yourself
to persist until you win

Chapter 2
Invest in Yourself

August sat on the back porch, sipping coffee and listening to the world wake up. A light breeze carried the faint scent of the sea, mingling with the aroma of fresh-cut grass from his neighbor's yard. The moment should have been peaceful, but August's mind was restless. His journal sat open on the small table beside him, yesterday's promise staring back at him in bold letters: *I promise myself.*

It was a start, but now what?

Oscar's words from the day before lingered like the faint hum of a melody. The Backyard Millionaire Creed felt solid, like a set of tracks for a train that was going somewhere. But this morning, it felt like he was staring down an empty line, unsure of where to begin.

The crunch of gravel announced Oscar's arrival before he stepped into view, a brown paper sack under one arm and a grin on his face. "Morning," he said, pulling up a chair without waiting for an invitation.

"Morning," August replied. "Coffee?"

"Already had mine," Oscar said, setting the sack on the table. "But I brought you something better."

Oscar reached into the bag and pulled out an old, dog-eared book. Its cover was faded, the title barely legible, but the weight of it seemed significant. He placed it in front of August with a thud.

"What's this?" August asked, picking it up.

"An investment," Oscar said simply.

August flipped through the pages, finding a mix of underlined passages, notes scrawled in the margins, and yellowed corners folded down. "Looks like you've had this a while."

"Since I was about your age," Oscar said. "That book taught me one of the most important lessons of my life—if you don't invest in yourself, don't expect anyone else to."

August set the book down. "What do you mean, 'invest in yourself'?"

Oscar leaned back, lacing his fingers behind his head. "It means taking the time, energy, and sometimes money to make yourself better. Smarter. Stronger. Wiser. People think of investments as something you do with stocks or real estate, but the greatest asset you'll ever have is you. You can't build wealth, happiness, or anything else worthwhile if you're not willing to put something into yourself first."

August considered that. He thought of all the time he'd spent chasing the next big thing, hoping for a shortcut to success. He'd invested in tools, courses, and ideas, but rarely in himself.

"So how do I do it?" he asked.

Oscar leaned forward, resting his elbows on the table. "Start small. Read something every day that challenges you. Take care of your body—exercise, eat well, get enough sleep. Learn a new skill, even if it doesn't seem immediately useful. And don't be afraid to spend money on things that will help you grow. Books, training, mentors—it's all part of the process."

August picked up the book again, running his fingers over its worn edges. "This book... it helped you?"

Oscar nodded. "More than I can tell you. Not because of what it taught me, but because it opened my eyes to something bigger. Every page felt like a conversation with someone who had already been where I wanted to go. It made me realize I wasn't alone in figuring this stuff out."

The words sank in, and August felt a flicker of excitement. Maybe he'd been going about this all wrong, focusing on what he didn't have instead of building up what he did.

"I guess I've never thought of myself as an investment," he admitted.

Oscar grinned. "Most people don't. They spend their whole lives putting their money and energy into things that won't last. Cars, gadgets, quick wins. But you? You're the only investment guaranteed to pay off—if you're willing to do the work."

August nodded, feeling a spark of clarity. He turned to the first page of the book and began to read, the words pulling him in.

Oscar stood, brushing off his jeans. "I'll leave you to it," he said. "Just remember—every minute you spend investing in yourself is a minute well spent. It's the one thing no one can ever take away from you."

As Oscar walked back toward his truck, August kept reading. The sun climbed higher in the sky, but he didn't notice. For the first time in a long time, he felt like he wasn't stuck. He was building something, one word, one page, one day at a time.

At the top of his journal, he wrote: *I promise myself to invest in me.*

And as the morning stretched on, August felt a quiet confidence settle over him. He wasn't just chasing his dreams anymore—he was building the foundation to hold them.

The Backyard Millionaire Creed

Promise yourself

To invest in yourself

To honor your instincts

To never invest on
an emotional basis

To negotiate with
win/win in mind

To find a need and fill it

Promise yourself
to persist until you win

Chapter 3
Honor Your Instincts

August stood at the edge of a construction site, watching the workers pour concrete for the foundation of a new building. The smell of wet cement hung heavy in the air, mingling with the rhythmic thud of tools and machinery. He'd come here for inspiration, hoping that seeing someone else's vision take shape might help his own feel less out of reach.

But all it did was remind him of how far he still had to go.

"Looks solid, doesn't it?"

The familiar voice pulled August out of his thoughts. Oscar stood a few feet away, hands in his pockets, surveying the scene with a quiet confidence.

"It does," August said, nodding toward the workers. "I can't imagine how many decisions go into something like this. One bad call, and the whole thing could fall apart."

Oscar stepped closer, a knowing smile on his face. "That's why you've got to trust the people who know what they're doing. And why they've got to trust themselves. Foundations aren't built on second-guessing."

August smirked. "Is this about the construction site, or are we about to have another life lesson?"

Oscar chuckled. "Both." He tilted his head toward the freshly poured concrete. "This right here—this is like your instincts. It's the foundation you build everything else on. If you don't trust it, the whole thing crumbles."

Oscar unfolded the worn copy of the Millionaire Creed, and tapped the next line with his finger.

August crossed his arms, his skepticism evident. "You really think instincts are that reliable? What if you're wrong?"

Oscar looked at him, his expression serious. "You ever hear of analysis paralysis?"

August nodded. "Overthinking everything to the point you don't do anything."

"Exactly," Oscar said. "People get so caught up in trying to make the perfect decision that they end up making none at all. But your instincts? They're faster than your logic. They cut through the noise and give you the answer you already know deep down. The trick is learning to listen to them."

August leaned against a nearby stack of lumber, considering Oscar's words. He thought about the times he'd ignored that little voice in his head, only to regret it later.

"Alright," he said, "but how do you know when it's your instincts talking and not just fear or wishful thinking?"

Oscar smiled. "That's the hard part. It takes practice. Start small. Pay attention to that gut feeling when you're making everyday decisions. The more you trust it, the sharper it gets. And when it's something big, don't ignore it—even if it doesn't make sense at first."

August thought back to their first meeting at the hardware store. He had resisted Oscar's advice back then, convinced he knew better. But something about Oscar's presence had tugged at him, even then. It wasn't logic that made him listen—it was instinct.

"You think instincts ever steer you wrong?" August asked.

Oscar shrugged. "Not often. But when they do, it's usually because you're ignoring something else—like facts or common sense. Instincts aren't a substitute for thinking; they're a tool. You've just got to learn when to use them."

The sound of a truck backing up punctuated the air, and August watched as workers smoothed the wet concrete, making it level and even.

"You know," Oscar continued, "most people don't trust their instincts because they're afraid of being wrong. But you can't build anything—whether it's a building, a business, or a life—if you're too scared to make a decision."

August nodded slowly. "So it's about confidence."

"Confidence," Oscar agreed, "and being willing to learn from your mistakes. Even when your instincts lead you wrong, they teach you something. But ignoring them? That's the real mistake."

August turned back to the site, watching the workers move with purpose and precision. The foundation wasn't just a starting point; it was the most important part of the building. Without it, nothing else could stand.

For the first time, the connection between instincts and progress made sense. His gut wasn't just a reaction—it was a guide, a blueprint he hadn't been using.

When he got home that evening, August opened his journal. Beneath yesterday's entry, he wrote: *I promise myself to honor my instincts.*

He thought about how many times he had ignored them, how often he had doubted that quiet inner voice. But not anymore. From now on, he would trust himself to know what to do, even when the path wasn't clear.

Because just like the foundation of a building, his instincts were what everything else would stand on.

The Backyard Millionaire Creed

Promise yourself

To invest in yourself

To honor your instincts

To never invest on an emotional basis

To negotiate with win/win in mind

To find a need and fill it

Promise yourself
to persist until you win

Chapter 4

Never Invest on an Emotional Basis

The diner was quiet, the kind of calm that came between the breakfast rush and the lunchtime crowd. August sat in a corner booth, nursing a cup of coffee. He wasn't hungry; he'd come here for the noise of other people's conversations, hoping it would drown out the thoughts swirling in his head.

Spread across the table were papers: bank statements, property listings, and notes he'd scribbled late into the night. It was all part of the same obsession that had kept him up for weeks. There was a property he couldn't stop thinking about—a fixer-upper on the edge of town. It wasn't practical. It wasn't even a good deal, but something about it had latched onto his brain like a song he couldn't shake.

The sound of the door opening got his attention. Oscar stepped inside, scanning the room before spotting August. Without hesitation, he made his way to the booth and slid into the seat across from him.

"I thought I might find you here," Oscar said, nodding toward the papers. "What's all this?"

August sighed, shuffling the documents into a messy pile. "I'm trying to figure out if I should go for it. There's this house...it's not a great deal, but I can't stop thinking about it. I feel like I'd regret it if I don't at least try."

Oscar leaned back, his eyes narrowing as he considered August's words. "Sounds like your emotions are driving the bus right now."

August frowned. "What's wrong with that? Isn't passion part of making big decisions?"

Oscar shook his head, a small smile tugging at the corner of his mouth. "Passion's good, but it's not a strategy. Investing on emotion is like betting on a horse because you like its name. You might get lucky once, but luck isn't how you build wealth—or anything that lasts."

August bristled. "It's not just emotion. I've run the numbers. I think it could work."

"Do you *know* it'll work, or are you trying to convince yourself?" Oscar asked, his voice steady but firm.

August didn't answer. He hated how easily Oscar could cut through his defenses.

Oscar reached across the table and tapped the stack of papers. "Here's the thing, August: emotions make you impulsive. They cloud your judgment. When it comes to investing—whether it's money, time, or energy—you can't let feelings make the decisions for you. You've got to step back and look at the facts."

August folded his arms, staring out the window. "So what are you saying? I should just walk away?"

Oscar shook his head. "I'm saying you should ask yourself the right questions. Does this deal make sense on paper? Does it align with your long-term goals? Or are you chasing it because you're afraid of missing out?"

The words hit harder than August wanted to admit. He'd been so focused on the idea of the house—the potential, the dream—that he hadn't stopped to think about whether it actually fit into the bigger picture.

Oscar leaned forward, his tone softening. "Listen, it's not about killing your excitement. It's about channeling it into something solid.

When you take emotion out of the equation, you see things for what they really are. And sometimes, that clarity will save you from a bad decision."

August let the words sink in, staring at the papers on the table. He thought about the times he'd let excitement get the better of him—opportunities that seemed perfect in the moment but turned out to be mistakes.

"So how do you know when it's the right move?" he asked finally.

Oscar smiled. "That's the beauty of it. When the numbers make sense and your instincts align, you'll know. But you've got to be patient enough to wait for that clarity. Emotional decisions might feel good in the moment, but logical ones will feel good for a lifetime."

The waitress came by and refilled August's coffee. He thanked her quietly, staring into the dark liquid as if it held answers. Slowly, he began gathering the papers, stacking them neatly.

"I guess I've got some thinking to do," he said.

Oscar nodded, sliding out of the booth. "That's all I'm asking. Don't make a decision until you're sure it's the right one—not just the exciting one."

As Oscar walked toward the door, August watched him go, the words from the creed echoing in his mind: *Never invest on an emotional basis.*

When he got home that afternoon, August opened his journal. He stared at the blank page for a long time before writing: *I promise myself to think before I leap. Emotions are valuable, but they don't make the best business partners.*

He put the pen down and leaned back, feeling the weight of clarity settle over him. The house wasn't off the table—not yet—but he would make his decision the right way this time.

Because building a life worth living wasn't about chasing every opportunity. It was about knowing which ones were worth the risk.

The Backyard Millionaire Creed

Promise yourself

To invest in yourself

To honor your instincts

To never invest on
an emotional basis

**To negotiate with
win/win in mind**

To find a need and fill it

Promise yourself
to persist until you win

Chapter 5
Negotiate with Win/Win in Mind

The beach was quiet except for the rhythmic crash of waves against the shore. August walked alongside Oscar, the sand shifting beneath their feet. The conversation had started casually, but as always, Oscar seemed to know exactly when to steer things deeper.

"Negotiation," Oscar said, picking up a small, smooth rock and tossing it into the surf, "is one of the most misunderstood skills in the world."

August kept his gaze on the horizon. "Because people think it's about winning?"

"Exactly," Oscar replied, brushing sand from his hands. "Most people approach it like a competition—who can get the better deal, who can walk away with more. But that kind of thinking? It's shortsighted. Real negotiation isn't about winning or losing. It's about finding a way for everyone to win."

August tilted his head, considering the words. "But isn't that idealistic? In a lot of deals, someone has to give up something, right?"

Oscar shook his head. "Not necessarily. The best negotiators don't take—they create. They find ways to meet their own goals while helping the other person meet theirs. That's a win/win. And when you can do that, you're not just closing a deal—you're building a relationship, a foundation for future opportunities."

August stopped to skip a rock across the water, watching it hop three times before disappearing beneath the waves. "So how do you know when it's win/win? What if the other person just takes advantage of you?"

Oscar smiled. "It's not about being a pushover. It's about being smart. You've got to do your homework—know what you want, what the other person values, and what the boundaries are. A win/win doesn't mean giving up what's important to you. It means finding creative ways to align both sides' interests. The key is to listen more than you talk."

August frowned. "What if the other person isn't willing to play fair?"

Oscar shrugged. "Then you walk away. Not every deal is worth making. The beauty of negotiating with win/win in mind is that you can do it with integrity. If someone isn't willing to meet you there, it's not the right deal."

The two continued walking, the sound of their steps blending with the surf. August thought about how he had approached negotiations in the past—how often he had been too focused on what he wanted to consider the bigger picture.

"Here's something to remember," Oscar said, stopping to pick up another rock. "When you make someone feel like they've won, they'll want to work with you again. Trust and goodwill are worth more than any single deal. They're what keep the opportunities coming."

August nodded, the words settling into his mind like pieces of a puzzle he hadn't been able to fit together before.

That evening, as he sat at his desk, he opened his journal and wrote: *I promise myself to negotiate with win/win in mind. Trust and relationships are my greatest currency.*

And for the first time, negotiation didn't feel like a battle. It felt like an art.

The Backyard Millionaire Creed

Promise yourself

To invest in yourself

To honor your instincts

To never invest on
an emotional basis

To negotiate with
win/win in mind

To find a need and fill it

Promise yourself
to persist until you win

Chapter 6
Find a Need and Fill It

The farmer's market was alive with energy. Brightly colored tents lined the gravel lot, and the scent of freshly baked bread mingled with the sharp tang of sea salt carried on the breeze. August walked past tables overflowing with ripe produce, jars of honey, and handmade soaps. The hum of conversation and the occasional burst of laughter added to the lively atmosphere.

Oscar strolled beside him, carrying a small paper bag filled with fresh apples. He tossed one to August, who caught it with a smirk. "Feel that energy?" Oscar asked, taking a bite of his own apple.

"It's impressive," August admitted. "Feels like the whole town's here."

Oscar nodded, gesturing toward a booth where a woman sold bouquets of wildflowers, her hands moving quickly to arrange blooms for a waiting customer. "Every person here is solving a problem, August. They're meeting needs."

"Needs?" August said, glancing around.

Oscar stopped walking and pointed to a nearby table piled high with homemade pastries. "Take that guy, for instance. He's not just selling bread—he's giving people a taste of something homemade, something they don't have the time or skill to make themselves. That's a need."

They continued walking, passing a young couple selling hand-carved wooden utensils. "Those two," Oscar said, motioning toward the booth. "They saw a gap in the market. People want something unique, something with character. So they're filling that need."

August tossed the apple back to Oscar. "So, what are you saying? Everything is just about solving problems?"

Oscar smiled. "Exactly. At its core, that's all business is. People need something—convenience, connection, quality—and a good entrepreneur steps in to fill that need. The best opportunities aren't complicated. They're just waiting for someone to notice."

August looked around, trying to see the market through Oscar's eyes. A woman handed a jar of jam to a customer, smiling as they exchanged money. A man in a straw hat adjusted the price signs on his baskets of fresh vegetables. Everywhere he turned, someone was offering something useful, something valuable.

"So how do you figure out what people need?" August asked.

Oscar leaned against a nearby post, chewing thoughtfully on his apple. "You start by listening. Pay attention to what people complain about, what they wish existed, what they say they don't have time for. Needs are everywhere, August. Most people just aren't paying attention."

August considered that. How often had he focused on his own goals without thinking about what others might need? "What if the need isn't obvious?" he asked.

Oscar grinned. "Then you dig a little deeper. Ask questions. Watch how people behave. A lot of times, people don't even know what they need until someone offers it to them. The trick is to care enough to notice."

They stopped at a booth selling hand-stitched aprons. The vendor greeted them warmly, explaining how she'd started her business after realizing how many home cooks wanted something practical but beautiful. "I couldn't find one I liked, so I made my own," she said with a laugh.

As they walked away, August glanced at Oscar. "She found a need and filled it."

Oscar smiled. "Now you're getting it."

Later that evening, as August sat at his kitchen table, the memory of the bustling market still fresh in his mind, he opened his journal. At the top of the page, he wrote: *I promise myself to find a need and fill it. The best opportunities are the ones that solve problems.*

He leaned back in his chair, feeling a quiet sense of clarity. The secret to success wasn't about reinventing the wheel. It was about paying attention, caring enough to serve, and offering something that mattered to the people around him.

And for the first time, he felt like he wasn't just chasing success—he was learning how to create it.

The Backyard Millionaire Creed

Promise yourself

To invest in yourself

To honor your instincts

To never invest on
an emotional basis

To negotiate with
win/win in mind

To find a need and fill it

**Promise yourself
to persist until you win**

Chapter 7
Persist Until You Win

The trail was steep, winding its way through a dense forest of spruce and birch. August's legs burned with every step, his breath coming in short, sharp bursts. He adjusted the strap of his backpack and glanced at Oscar, who walked a few paces ahead with the kind of ease that made it seem like the incline didn't exist.

"This was your idea of a good time?" August called out, half-joking, half-exhausted.

Oscar glanced over his shoulder with a grin. "The best views don't come easy."

August muttered something under his breath but kept climbing. They'd been on the trail for over an hour, and though the occasional break in the trees offered glimpses of the valley below, the summit still felt impossibly far away.

As they rounded another bend, Oscar slowed, letting August catch up. "You know," Oscar said, "a lot of people quit right about now."

"Right about now sounds pretty tempting," August admitted.

Oscar chuckled. "That's the difference between people who succeed and people who don't. Most give up when the climb gets hard. They don't realize how close they are to the top."

August stopped to catch his breath, leaning against a tree. "Yeah, but what if the top isn't worth it? What if you're climbing the wrong mountain?"

Oscar leaned on his hiking pole, his expression serious. "That's a fair question. But here's the thing—every climb teaches you something. Even if this isn't the mountain you want to stay on, the strength you build here will help you on the next one. The only way you lose is if you stop climbing altogether."

August nodded, wiping sweat from his brow. "Easy for you to say. You've already made it."

Oscar raised an eyebrow. "Made it? August, I'm still climbing. Always will be. The difference is, I've learned to enjoy the process. Success isn't just about reaching the top. It's about who you become on the way up."

The words hung in the air as August adjusted his pack and took a deep breath. He knew Oscar was right. Every time he'd faced a challenge in the past, it had felt impossible—until it wasn't. And every time, he'd come out stronger on the other side.

"Alright," August said, straightening up. "Let's keep going."

Oscar smiled and turned back to the trail, setting a steady pace.

By the time they reached the summit, August's legs felt like jelly, but the view stole his breath. The valley stretched out in every direction, the river snaking through lush green fields, and the sky a brilliant shade of blue. It was worth every step.

Oscar sat on a rock, pulling a water bottle from his pack. "See what I mean?"

August nodded, still catching his breath. "Yeah. You were right."

Oscar laughed. "You'll get used to saying that."

They sat in silence for a while, the wind tugging at their jackets, the climb already fading into memory.

"You know," Oscar said finally, "persistence isn't just about sticking it out when things get hard. It's about believing—really believing—

that what you're working toward is worth it. When you have that, nothing can stop you."

August looked out over the valley, the weight of the moment settling in. He thought about all the times he'd been tempted to quit—when progress felt too slow, or obstacles seemed too big. But every time, he'd found a way forward.

That night, as he sat at his desk, he opened his journal and wrote: *I promise myself to persist until I win. Every step brings me closer to who I'm meant to be.*

He leaned back, the words sinking in. Success wasn't about shortcuts or luck. It was about showing up, every single day, and refusing to quit—even when the trail seemed endless.

Because the best views really didn't come easy. And that made them all the more worth it.

The Backyard Millionaire Creed

Promise yourself

To invest in yourself

To honor your instincts

To never invest on
an emotional basis

To negotiate with
win/win in mind

To find a need and fill it

Promise yourself
to persist until you win

Chapter 8
The Journey Unfolds Perfectly

The evening sky was painted in soft hues of orange and pink, the last rays of sunlight reflecting off the calm surface of the bay. August and Oscar sat on a weathered bench overlooking the water, the kind of spot that begged for reflection. The quiet rhythm of the tide filled the space between them, unspoken words carried on the breeze.

August rested his elbows on his knees, hands clasped, and stared at the horizon. "It's funny," he said finally. "When I started all this, I thought success was about speed. About getting there as fast as I could."

Oscar didn't reply right away, letting the weight of the moment settle. "And now?"

"Now I get it," August said. "It's not about the destination. It's about the journey. Every step—even the ones that felt like detours or dead ends—was exactly what I needed."

Oscar nodded. "That's the thing most people don't realize until it's too late. Life isn't a straight line. It's a winding road, full of lessons disguised as setbacks and opportunities hidden in plain sight. The trick is to trust that it's all unfolding exactly as it should."

August leaned back against the bench, the tension in his shoulders easing. "I used to get so frustrated when things didn't go the way I planned. Like I was wasting time, or worse, going backward. But now I see it—every challenge, every delay—it was all part of the process."

Oscar smiled. "You know, when I met you at the hardware store, you were so determined to do things your way that you almost missed the chance to learn something new. But that stubbornness? It's part of what makes you who you are. You just had to learn to aim it in the right direction."

August chuckled, shaking his head. "I didn't make it easy on you, did I?"

"No," Oscar said with a laugh. "But that's what made it worth it. Watching you figure it out—watching you grow—has been one of the best parts of my journey."

They sat in comfortable silence for a while, the waves lapping at the shore.

"What's next?" August asked, his voice quiet.

Oscar looked at him, his expression thoughtful. "Next? You keep going. You take everything you've learned—every promise you've made to yourself—and you build on it. This isn't the end, August. It's just the beginning."

August nodded, the weight of the words settling in. He thought about the creed, how each plank had shaped him, pushing him to think differently, act differently, *be* different. He thought about the promises he had written in his journal, the ones he had kept and the ones he had struggled with.

For the first time, he wasn't afraid of the future. He wasn't worried about the timing, the obstacles, or even the inevitable setbacks. He understood now that life wasn't a race to some distant finish line. It was a series of moments, each one unfolding perfectly, leading him exactly where he was meant to be.

As the sun dipped below the horizon, August turned to Oscar. "Thanks. For everything."

Oscar smiled, his eyes crinkling at the corners. "Don't thank me. You're the one who did the work. I just pointed the way."

That night, August sat at his desk, the journal open in front of him. He picked up his pen and wrote: *I promise myself to trust the process. Life is unfolding exactly as it should.*

He set the pen down, a quiet sense of peace washing over him. For the first time, he wasn't chasing success—he was living it.

And as he closed the journal, he realized that the journey wasn't just about building wealth or achieving goals. It was about becoming the kind of person who could.

Promise Yourself

_____

_____

_____

_____

_____

_____

_____

_____

_____

_____

_____

_____

_____

Invest in yourself

_____

_____

_____

_____

_____

_____

_____

_____

_____

_____

_____

_____

_____

Honor your instincts

_____

_____

_____

_____

_____

_____

_____

_____

_____

_____

_____

_____

_____

Never invest on an emotional basis

_____

_____

_____

_____

_____

_____

_____

_____

_____

_____

_____

_____

Negotiate with win/win in mind

Find a need and fill it

_____

_____

_____

_____

_____

_____

_____

_____

_____

_____

_____

_____

_____

Promise yourself to persist until you win

_____

_____

_____

_____

_____

_____

_____

_____

_____

_____

_____

_____

_____

_____

_____

Dear Reader,

THANK YOU!

Your time is far more valuable than the modest price you paid for this short book. That you chose to invest your time here means the world to me, and I am deeply grateful for it. Time, after all, is the most precious resource we have—and how we spend it shapes everything.

It was an investment made in me over thirty years ago that still resonates, one that keeps me returning to the characters of August and Oscar. The man who made that investment was Chuck—Charles Hough. He wasn't a relative, and he had no clue who I was, just a passing stranger who left an indelible mark on my life.

Chuck was visiting family in my hometown of Homer, Alaska, when he wandered into the hardware store where I worked. He was unassuming, with the quiet confidence of someone who had built his own success. When our conversation turned to real estate—a topic that fascinated me even then—he asked a few questions. He learned I was deeply interested but hadn't graduated high school. I remember his thoughtful pause, the way he seemed to weigh what he was about to say.

The next day, Chuck came back to the store, carrying a book. It wasn't wrapped or ceremoniously presented, just handed to me like a gift from someone who saw potential where I hadn't yet.

"This," he said, holding it out to me, "is the only degree you'll ever need if you're serious about real estate."

The book was *The Buy and Hold Real Estate Strategy* by Dr. David Schumacher. I'll never forget what Chuck told me next: "If you read this book and really take it to heart, it'll be the equivalent of a four-year college degree."

And I believed him. I didn't just read the book—I *devoured* it. I absorbed every principle, every example, every hard-won piece of wisdom. That book changed the trajectory of my life. To this day, it holds a place of honor on my bookshelf, its pages worn and its lessons etched into my soul.

Chuck's belief in me lit a spark, but he wasn't the only one. Oscar, as a character, is an amalgamation of real mentors in my life, each of whom poured belief into me when I couldn't yet find it within myself. Foremost among them is my father, Norm Story.

My dad believed in me in a way that was tangible. He didn't just encourage me with words—though he often did—but he *loaned* me his belief when mine faltered. When I was ready to make my first real estate investment, he backed me up. Not financially, but emotionally. He made me feel like I couldn't fail, and because of that, I didn't. That first investment in my own backyard became the cornerstone of what would eventually grow into a small fortune.

These lessons, this *code*—or creed—is my way of passing along that same belief. My hope is that as you read this book, you'll feel what I felt all those years ago: the spark of possibility. I want you to know that you are capable of far more than you may believe today.

Promise yourself this: to believe in yourself, even when it feels impossible. And if you can't find that belief just yet, borrow it from someone else—whether it's from me, these pages, or a mentor in your life. You are worth it.

If you truly live by this code, you won't just succeed—you'll transform. And as you do, you'll find that the journey to becoming your best self is the greatest investment you'll ever make.

About the Author

CHRIS STORY resides in Homer, Alaska. He is an author, speaker, real estate investor, and owner/Broker of Story Real Estate, as well as host of the Backyard Millionaire Radio Show (podcast available on iTunes and Spotify).

Chris is a lifelong Alaskan, married to his high school sweetheart, Tiffanie. Together they have raised their two daughters, Ashley and Zoe in Homer, Alaska.

Connect with Chris

Chris Story
1005 Carriage Court
Homer Alaska 99603
(907)299.7653
Email: AlaskaMattersRadio@gmail.com

Made in the USA
Monee, IL
27 May 2025

17927723R00049